to dance

To Mom, for supporting my passion, and
To Mark, for helping me tell it
—S. C. S.

To Richard Jackson, my Captain
—M. S.

to dance

a memoir by **Siena Cherson Siegel**

with artwork by **Mark Siegel**

Atheneum Books for Young Readers New York London Toronto Sydney New Delhi

FLAT FEET

Big, empty spaces always made me dance.

A long hallway or a parking lot just begged for dance...

...like it wanted to be filled...

and I wanted to put dance in it.

A big, empty space was always an invitation.

I lived in San Juan, Puerto Rico, then.

When I was six, I was taken to the doctor, and the doctor told my mother that I had flat feet.

He said there was nothing that could be done about flat feet and not to even bother trying to fix flat feet.

What about some dance classes for her?

No, no, that won't help. Forget it.

DANCE CLASSES!!

Mommy, can I try anyway?

Yes, let's try anyway.

So she signed me up for dance classes.

I was too young for real ballet, but in class we moved around and did gymnastics.

DYING SWAN

When I was nine, my family moved to the Boston area for a year. I took classes with Mrs. Alcalde, who had a little dance studio in her basement.

I liked her.

We all had these white chiffon skirts. I liked those, too.

Children!

I have some great news! The **BOLSHOI** is coming to Boston!

The **BOLSHOI BALLET** toured America, from Russia. I went to see them perform with Mommy, Daddy, and my brother, Adam. The great **MAYA PLISETSKAYA** starred in it.

All I could think of for days after the performance was Maya Plisetskaya as the dying swan.

The part of the dying swan doesn't involve a lot of twirling or hard steps—it wasn't that.

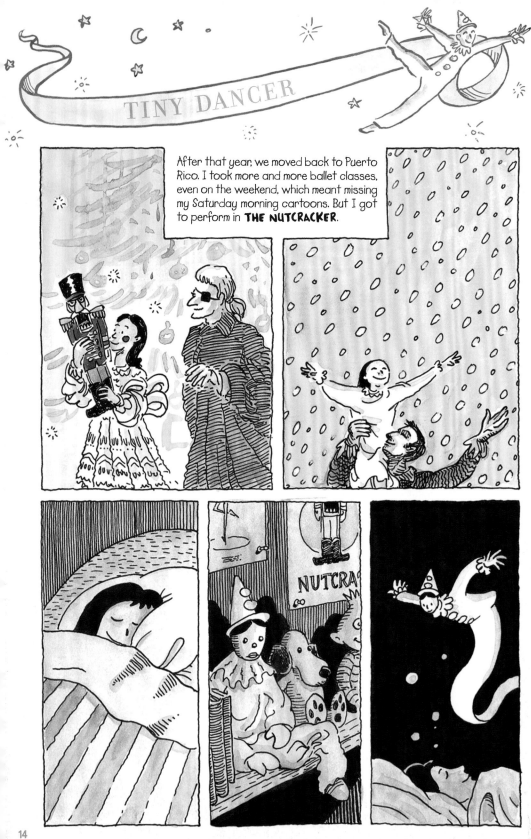

TINY DANCER

After that year, we moved back to Puerto Rico. I took more and more ballet classes, even on the weekend, which meant missing my Saturday morning cartoons. But I got to perform in **THE NUTCRACKER**.

NUTCRA

That summer, I flew to New York with my family for the American Ballet Theatre summer program and started to get a taste of the hard work of dancing.

Some days I felt like I couldn't hold my legs up anymore.

That was 1977, the year of the blackout.

CLICK!

A new book came out around then.

It was all about a little girl at the School of American Ballet, here in New York.

I read that book over and over and over. I studied the pictures.

There in those pages was where I wanted to be and what I wanted to do—it was that.

Exactly.

Bare Legs

A movie came out called **THE CHILDREN OF THEATRE STREET**. It was filmed at the **KIROV** school, in Leningrad.

It showed the fire of ballet being passed from one generation of dancers to another. They took dance very seriously in Russia.

Something struck me.

The little girls in the classes, they wore leotards and ballet shoes—but they didn't wear tights.

They only started wearing them later.

These little girls all had bare legs.

Those legs! I'd never seen anything like them. They looked like REAL dancer legs, strong, beautiful, grown-up legs on girls who were no older than me.

aUDITION

The next year, when I was eleven, we went back to New York so I could have an audition at the School of American Ballet, or **SAB** for short.

The audition was a private appointment.

There were three people in the room: me, the pianist, and Madame Tumkovsky.

And that was all. It was very simple.

Madame Tumkovsky wanted to see whether my body was suited to ballet and if I could move, if I was musical.

My family decided to move to New York for good, so I could go to the school.

After staying in a hotel on East 86th, we moved into an apartment on West 66th.

I didn't see Daddy very much anymore. He was back in San Juan a lot. At the time, I thought it was for his work.

I went to regular school during the day

and a few days a week, after school, I walked over to my ballet classes.

At the time, SAB was in the Juilliard building in **LINCOLN CENTER**, only one block away from home . . .

Once inside the big glass doors, it was no longer Juilliard.

Here, some of the greatest ballet dancers in the world walked around and took classes with some special teacher.

Little girls and big girls . . .

КОМ

I had stepped into a whole different world.

ПЬЕ

It didn't even feel like New York anymore.

КОМЕДИЯ МАСОК

Here I was, in the most famous ballet school in America . . . and it was Little Russia!

George Balanchine, who founded SAB, had come from Russia, from the Kirov school I'd seen in **THE CHILDREN OF THEATRE STREET**.

Mister Balanchine created SAB with an American named Lincoln Kirstein to train people to dance in his company, **NEW YORK CITY BALLET**.

For every year in school, you had to wear a colored leotard for the level you were in.

The girl in **A VERY YOUNG DANCER** wore forest green leotards for the fourth children's division, which is where I was placed.

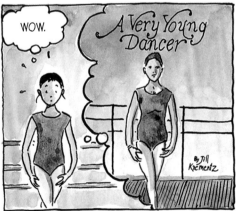

WOW.

A Very Young Dancer

By Jill Krementz

MY FIRST TOE SHOES

Every class started the same: **AT THE BARRE**.

Each of us was assigned a spot, arranged by height.

We practiced the same steps every time, day after day, week afer week, month after month.

Daddy arrived the next afternoon. He could only stay for two weeks.

Sienita!

How would you like your own barre?

He made the other half of my bedroom into a ballet studio with my own little barre and mirror.

For the mirror, he had to use lots of small squares. It turned out a little strange, but I loved it.

At Capezio's, someone named Judy Weiss made sure we got exactly the right fit for our first toe shoes.

After class one day,

on the huge black door to the dressing room was a piece of paper that gave the name of a ballet and a list of people.

Mister Balanchine choreographed many ballets with parts for children.

That day we found out who had been cast in this ballet.

And all the children were from the school.

I looked down the list, and there was my name!

Not everyone was selected.

We began to have rehearsals on top of classes, for one ballet after another:

COPPELIA...

THE NUTCRACKER...

A MIDSUMMER NIGHT'S DREAM.

BARYSHNIKOV!

Mister B. must be a big deal!

We were now rehearsing **HARLEQUINADE**, one of Mister B.'s earlier ballets, which he specially revived for Baryshnikov.

That piece would become my favorite.

The characters all come from La Commedia Dell'Arte.

Harlequin...

Columbine...

Pierrot...

There were four little Pierrots and four little Pierrettes.

That first season, I got to be a Pierrette.

BackStage!

When it was almost time for opening night, we moved into the New York State Theater.

All the dress rehearsals were there, and so were the performances.

Backstage was a whole world to explore between rehearsals. We discovered all kinds of things.

We discovered that ballerinas wander around in beautiful Japanese robes when they aren't dancing.

So, naturally we had to have our own, so we could go wandering.

We loved the dressing rooms.

SUZANNE FARRELL

MERRILL ASHLEY

We hoped one of the doors would open, just then.

The principal dancers were everywhere, though.

You never knew who might step into the elevator with you.

DING!

Like BARYSHNIKOV, who always smiled and spoke with a thick Russian accent.

Hi, gyorls!

DING!

Sigh.

Aaah!

Misha!

We rehearsed and rehearsed.

Then we'd perform what we'd been rehearsing all these months—on stage.

This was LINCOLN CENTER! There would be **THOUSANDS** of people in the audience!

It's true, what they say about the butterflies.

Nerves feel like butterflies fluttering in your stomach, every time.

Your heart beats fast. You're breathing harder. It's very hard to stand still.

MISTER B.

Mommy saw me as a Pierrette four times. But Daddy didn't get to see it at all.

In performances, during the scenes when we weren't dancing on stage, a lot of the other girls liked to stay in the dressing room, where they played jacks and had fun.

But I went up by myself, to watch.

You had to stand in the very front part of the wing against the black curtain. It was VERY important the audience didn't see you.

I loved to watch from the wings.

Here I was, watching **SUZANNE FARRELL**.

Every time I went up there, I saw Mister B. in the other wing across from me.

He always watched from the front wing, stage right.

After the performance, we left through the stage door, back to our lives.

You hungry?

Yeah!

Wanna get some pecan pie?

The next day, it was back to school, back to ballet class, back to the barre. We'd stand in our same places, now in our burgundy leotards, next to the same person we've always stood next to, and did our pliés and our tendus again and again.

It went on like this for my first two years at SAB.

SIR DUKE

Adam also taught me how to do two different things with different hands, like how drummers do one rhythm with one hand and another with the other hand at the same time.

WITH A VOICE

LIKE ELLA'S

RINGING OUT

THERE'S NO WAY

THAT THE

BAND CAN LOSE

After a couple of years in New York, ballet classes intensified.

They were now after school every day of the week.

And Saturdays.

Several days a week, ballet started at 2:30, so they arranged my schedule at school to let me leave early.

That year, for vacation, I left on a trip to Florida with Adam and my father.

We went to a Miami Dolphins game. Even watching football, I saw ballet.

A dancer needs so much training, so much strength.

You get hurt, injured, bashed...

transformed.

A dancer needs so much work on timing, positions, line...

technique, execution, coordination.

And then . . .

And then it all comes together for a fleeting moment of magic when you find yourself doing the impossible.

We also saw my father's relatives there, for dinner.

Her boobs are huge!

It runs in my family!

Oh no. What if mine keep growing and growing and growing!

You really can't be a ballet dancer and have huge breasts!

I thought maybe I should tie gauze around them at night, hoping that might contain them a bit at least.

DANCING SPIRITS

I was hungry for every kind of dance.

I started filling myself up with as much dance history and knowledge as possible, like world dances and old movie musicals.

Cyd Charisse...

Gene Kelly...

Fred Astaire...

And I spent hours at the Performing Arts Library on weekends, watching movies and archival videos.

Somewhere around this time I began taking class on Sunday...

By now, my feet were no longer flat.

I listened to music all the time. The Walkman was a new thing, then. Everyone had to have a Walkman.

They were heavy and expensive and kind of big. But I never went anywhere without mine.

I could bike around the park any day with my favorite music.

After dance classes on sunny Sundays I would meet all my friends from school at Sheep's Meadow.

This was my time to feel normal, doing what other teenagers do.

REFUGE

Now ballet classes started at 10:30 in the morning.

I had to switch to Professional Children's School, so I could take ballet classes all day.

I would go to and from PCS and SAB, one or two academic classes, and one or two ballet classes, and back . . .

Many of my friends from SAB did this too. We would walk back and forth together, and sometimes stop at one of their apartments for lunch, and then go to SAB.

Meanwhile Mom and Dad were divorcing.

There was no peace at home.

Dance class was the only time I could really get away from what was happening between my parents.

All the hard work at SAB became a relief for me, a refuge.

In spite of all its struggles, it was my peaceful time.

I was now sixteen.

Day by day, week by week, I worked and learned and deepened my training.

Besides Tumi and Suki Schorer I had other excellent teachers, including Stanley Williams and Alexandra Danilova.

GISELLE

Hey, Mandy! ABT is doing **GISELLE**. You wanna go with me?

What's **GISELLE**?

Oh, it's the best story ballet, and it's with Baryshnikov and Gelsey Kirkland.

She's my favorite!

What's the story?

Giselle is a peasant girl in a small village.

She loves to dance,

even though she shouldn't because of her bad heart.

Her heart?

Yeah, some kind of illness.

What kind of illness?

I don't know.

It doesn't matter.

So, one day a prince comes to the village, but he's disguised as a regular guy out hunting or something. He and Giselle meet, and they fall in love. But it turns out he's already engaged to someone else.

Uh-oh.

Yeah, and it gets worse. Giselle goes mad and she DIES. And that's the end of Act I.

Whoa.

In Act II, the prince goes to visit her grave in the forest. Every night the forest is full of Wilis, until daybreak.

Wilis?

Yeah, Wilis.

Is her love different than the other Wilis, who had their hearts broken?

PARTNERING CLASS

Partnering class was a whole new thing.

So far all your life in ballet, you're dancing by yourself, then suddenly you have to dance with somebody else.

Together you do different things than you can do on your own.

Some of it's really scary!

It's almost like starting all over again. All the things you were confident about, change.

Also, until then, all my classes had been just girls.

I now had several different partners.

One of them was my boyfriend at the time.

It was also really fun because it felt more like the kinds of things I had seen all my favorite dancers doing.

It suddenly felt very grown up doing partnering.

GOOD-BYE MISTER B.

The funeral was during the week. There were so many people there.

NYCB performed that night. Lincoln Kirstein came out in front of the curtain to say this was dedicated to Mister B.

"The performance must go on, he would have wanted that."

It ended with **SYMPHONY IN C.**

If they're going to do *Symphony in C,* it's always the **LAST** thing on the program, always.

Suzanne Farrell was dancing in the second movement, the slow movement.

I had seen her do it many, many times.

She was very, very beautiful in that part.

In the slow movement, Mister B. choreographed many backward falls for the ballerina . . .

with her hands above her head,

and the man catches her, over and over.

That night, when she did those falls, Suzanne Farrell crossed her arms over her chest as she was falling.

She danced his death.

Everyone knew this was her good-bye to Mister B.

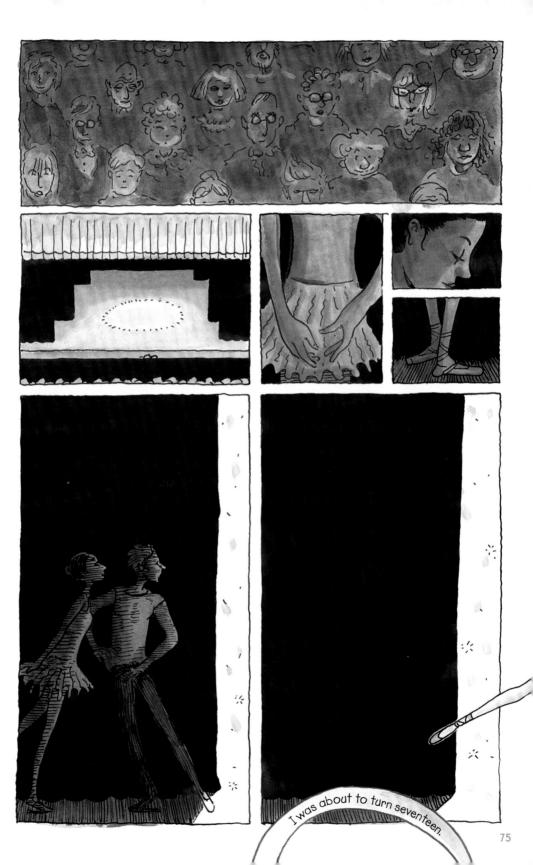

I was about to turn seventeen.

At eighteen I stopped dancing.

I had a terrible ankle injury the year before.

Instead I went to college,

a difficult and complete change for me,

but I needed to grow and develop in new ways.

And I did.

STATE THEATER
CENTER PLAZA
W 64th ST.. N. Y. C.

LEFT B 1
ENTER NOW SEAT
FOURTH RING $9.00
GOOD ONLY
FRI. EVE.
FRIDAY EVENING 17
8:00 P. M. 1978
PRICE $9.00 NEW YORK STATE THEATER

RK CITY BALLET
Program Subject to Change

from Siena's
scrapbook

I got autographs all over my Pierrot

Baryshnikov!

Nutcracker performance in San Juan.

EL NUEVO DIA—MARTES 20 DE FEBRERO DE 1979

27

ballet

En el New York City Ballet

Siena Cherson, quien estudió en la escuela de los Ballets de San Juan, ha estado apareciendo en la producción de los ballets "Coppelia", "Cascanueces" y "Herlequinade" del New York City Ballet en Lincoln Center, bajo la dirección de George Ballanchine, y con la participación de los bailarines Mikhail Baryshnikov, Peter Martins, Peter McBride y Suzanne Farrell. La presente temporada termina esta semana.

ción

la noche, será la
chie Torres, en la
posición consta de
la sala Oller de la

952. Tomó sus pri-
Carola Colom Co-
uy joven en varias
su cuarto año, se
el maestro Rafael Villa-
Greenwich Villa-

ció una beca para
artista regrese a
el círculo artístico
do ya varias expo-
y otros pueblos de
ca, Museo de Arte
Católica, Recinto
Padín y la Galería
chas exposiciones en
exposiciones en
y Venezuela.

se como impre-
ntiliano. Es cos-
obra tiene sabor
tros campos de
al para pinta-
las campiña-

BALLETS DE SAN JUAN
INSTITUTO DE CULTURA PUERTORRI
PRESENTA
GRAN TEMPORADA DE NAVIDAD
EL CASCANUE

Viernes
6
Enero
de 1978

TEATRO TAP

8:30 P.M. - $5

In the Puerto Ri newspaper!

7:05
Deportes con Tato Rivera (6)

Siena Cherson

SCHEDULE OF CLASSES

AMERICAN BALLET THEATRE SCHOOL

LEON DANIELIAN
Director

SUMMER 1977

3 WEST 61st STREET · NEW YORK, N.Y. 10023
(212) JUDSON 6 - 3355

	TIME	CLASS	INSTRUCTOR
M	X 10:00-11:30	Intermediate I	Merinowa
O	11:30- 1:00	Professional	Pereyaslavec
N	1:00- 2:30	Intermediate	Danielian
D	3:30- 3:00	Intermediate Pointe	Wilde
A	4:30- 6:00	Intermediate II	Merinowa
Y	6:00- 7:30	Intermediate	Clement
T	6:15- 7:15	Adult Beginner I	
U	X 10:00-11:30	Advanced	Merinowa
E	11:30- 1:00	Professional I	Pereyaslavec
S	1:00- 2:30	Professional	Danielian
D	3:00- 4:00	Pointe	Maule
A	3:30- 4:30	Children	Clement
Y	4:30- 6:00	Intermediate	Merinowa
	6:00- 7:30	Advanced	Pereyaslavec
W	X 10:00-11:30	Adult Beginner II	Danielian
E	11:30- 1:00	Intermediate	Wilde
D	1:30- 2:30	Professional	Merinowa
N	3:00- 3:00	Intermediate	Maule
E	4:30- 4:30	Variation	Clem
S	6:00- 7:30		

NEW YORK CITY BALLET

Backstage in our Japanese robes ←

Harlequins in the dressing room before going on stage ↗

COPPÉLIA—NOV. 17-1978

Harlequinade—Premiere Wed Nov. 22 1978

continued from page 42

ACT II

An Enchanted Park

Harlequin, Colombine, Pierrot, Pierrette, Les Sbires, Cassandre, Léandre, Les Scaramouches, La Bonne Fée, joined by

Ballabile des enfants:

Polichinelles   Tamara Molina-Aquire, Hilary Berlind, Maya Ciarrochi, Melissa Elstein, Katherine Healy, Aina Lakis, Heather Lem, Natalie Porat

Les Petits Harlequins   Nina Echegaray, Alexandra Ehrlich, Susan Hilferty, Wendi Maguire, Julie Michael, Nadine Miral, Lisa Peters, Maria Rogic

Pierrots et Pierrettes   Linda Altounian, Diedre Carberry, Siena Cherson, Julie Keisman, Diane Paulus, Danielle Tiletnick, Julie Tobiason, Katherine Weymouth

Scaramouches   Betsy Cooper, Allison Potter, Julie Ronsenbluth, Stephanie Rothenberger, Amy Stahl, Patricia Tomlinson, Tara Walsh, Kim Weild

Invités   Heléne Alexopoulos, Carole Divet, Susan Freedman, Victoria Hall, Jean Hauser, Lisa Hess, Dana Lewis,

continued from page 39

ACT II

Dr. Coppélius Secret Workshop

... a and Her Friends   Patricia McBride, and Bonita Borne, Elyse Borne, Judith Fugate, Lisa Hess, Elise Ingalls, Sandra Jennings, Lourdes Lopez, Sandra Zigars

Dr. Coppélius   Shaun O'Brien
Frantz   Helgi Tomasson
...s—Astrologer   Timothy Fox
Juggler   Christopher Fleming
Acrobat   Christopher d'Amboise
Chinaman   Douglas Hay

INTERMISSION

ACT III

...age Wedding and Festival of Bells

...rgomaster   William Johnson
...d Friends   Bonita Borne, Elyse Borne, Judith Fugate, Lisa Hess, Elise Ingalls, Sandra Jennings, Lourdes Lopez, Sandra Zigars Christopher d'Amboise, Corne... Peter Frame, Timothy Fox, Patrick Hinson, Bruce Padget...

...élius   Shaun O'Brien

...urs   Sheryl Ware and Tamara A... Linda Altounian, Hilary Be... Deirdre Carberry, Siena Ch... Nina Echegaray, Alexandr... Melissa Elstein, Elizabeth... Katherine Healy, Susan H... Aina Lakis, Heather Lem... Stephanie Lyon, Wendi... Julie Michael, Nadine... Mara Nedzela, Anasta... Allison Potter, Valerie... Marija Rogic, Candace...

When I got too tall to play Pierrette, I had to play Pierrot. With my friend Julie at dress rehearsal.

NUTCRACKER REHEARSAL SCHEDULE

NEW YORK CITY BALLET
Winter Season 1979-80

ALL REHEARSALS FOR THE LAST WEEK
ARE SUBJECT TO CHANGE OR MAY RUN OVER.
PLEASE KEEP YOURSELF FLEXIBLE.

TUESDAY, November 27
N.Y. State Theatre
Lower Concourse

WEDNESDAY
N.Y.
Main

PARTY SCENE A with Company
PARTY SCENE B with Company
Sadler, P. Taylor, J. White

THE NUTCRACKER
PERFORMANCE SCHEDULE

I always wrote in the lead dancer on my performance nights.

NEW YORK CITY BALLET
Winter Season 1979-80

B 24
ROW SEAT
CENTER $10.00
THIRD RING
RIGHT
1978
 OOD ONLY
SAT. MAT. 2
DECEMBER
NEW YORK STATE THEATER

SUNDAY MATINEE Kay Mazzo
SUNDAY EVENING Suzanne Farrell

TUESDAY EVENING Merrill Ashley   DECEMBER 2, 1979
THURSDAY EVENING Kay Mazzo   DECEMBER 2, 1979
SATURDAY MATINEE Elyse Bourne   DECEMBER 4, 1979
SATURDAY EVENING Merrill Ashley   DECEMBER 6, 1979

WEDNESDAY EVENING Farrell-Bonnie   DECEMBER 8, 1979
FRIDAY EVENING Elyse Borne   DECEMBER 8, 1979
SUNDAY MATINEE Judith Fugate Christin DECEMBER 12, 1979
SUNDAY MATINEE Kyra Nichols   DECEMBER 14, 1979

TUESDAY EVENING Maryoth Lavien   DECEMBER 16, 1979
THURSDAY EVENING Ashley-Kyra Nichols DECEMBER 16, 1979
SATURDAY EVENING Ashley-Stands   DECEMBER 18, 1979
SATURDAY MATINEE Ashley   DECEMBER 20, 1979
SATURDAY EVENING Nichols-Watts   DECEMBER 22, 1979

WEDNESDAY MATINEE Kyra Nichols   DECEMBER 22, 1979
WEDNESDAY EVENING Samandval-Saroh   DECEMBER 26, 1979
FRIDAY EVENING Kyra Nichols   DECEMBER 26, 1979
SUNDAY MATINEE Kyra Nichols   DECEMBER 28, 1979
SUNDAY EVENING Patty McBride-Tomas   DECEMBER 30, 1979
                Frohlich

MONDAY MATINEE Patty McBride-Tomas
Monday Evening   Frohlich

at 1:00 PM
at 5:00 PM

at 6:00 PM
at 6:00 PM
at 2:00 PM
at 8:00 PM

at 6:00 PM
at 8:00 PM
at 1:00 PM
at 5:00 PM

at 8:00 PM
at 6:00 PM
at 2:00 PM
at 8:00 PM

at 1:0

With Adam in my favorite
Miami Dolphins jersey.

Mark's first study for 'To Dance'!

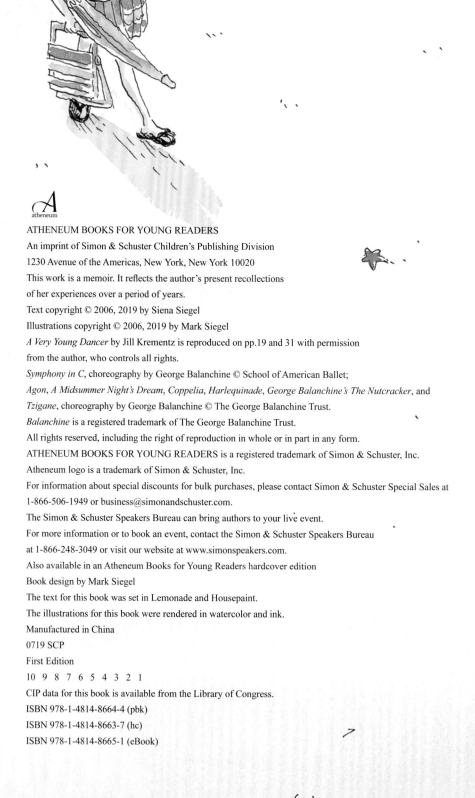

ATHENEUM BOOKS FOR YOUNG READERS

An imprint of Simon & Schuster Children's Publishing Division

1230 Avenue of the Americas, New York, New York 10020

This work is a memoir. It reflects the author's present recollections
of her experiences over a period of years.

Text copyright © 2006, 2019 by Siena Siegel

Illustrations copyright © 2006, 2019 by Mark Siegel

A Very Young Dancer by Jill Krementz is reproduced on pp.19 and 31 with permission
from the author, who controls all rights.

Symphony in C, choreography by George Balanchine © School of American Ballet;

Agon, A Midsummer Night's Dream, Coppelia, Harlequinade, George Balanchine's The Nutcracker, and
Tzigane, choreography by George Balanchine © The George Balanchine Trust.

Balanchine is a registered trademark of The George Balanchine Trust.

All rights reserved, including the right of reproduction in whole or in part in any form.

ATHENEUM BOOKS FOR YOUNG READERS is a registered trademark of Simon & Schuster, Inc.

Atheneum logo is a trademark of Simon & Schuster, Inc.

For information about special discounts for bulk purchases, please contact Simon & Schuster Special Sales at
1-866-506-1949 or business@simonandschuster.com.

The Simon & Schuster Speakers Bureau can bring authors to your live event.

For more information or to book an event, contact the Simon & Schuster Speakers Bureau
at 1-866-248-3049 or visit our website at www.simonspeakers.com.

Also available in an Atheneum Books for Young Readers hardcover edition

Book design by Mark Siegel

The text for this book was set in Lemonade and Housepaint.

The illustrations for this book were rendered in watercolor and ink.

Manufactured in China

0719 SCP

First Edition

10 9 8 7 6 5 4 3 2 1

CIP data for this book is available from the Library of Congress.

ISBN 978-1-4814-8664-4 (pbk)

ISBN 978-1-4814-8663-7 (hc)

ISBN 978-1-4814-8665-1 (eBook)

ACKNOWLEDGMENTS

Special thanks to Adam Cherson, Alexis Siegel, and Lee Wade; and many, many thanks to Ann Bobco, Tanya McKinnon, Rebecca Wright, Yuri Kucherov, Kristy Raffensberger, Sonia Chaghatzbanian, Michael McCartney, Jeannie Ng, and Emma Dryden; and for this Special Edition, thank you to the excellent Reka Simonsen, Julia McCarthy, Greg Stadnyk, Karyn Lee, and Clare McGlade!

A deep, special thank you to the 2007 Sibert Committee members:
Chair Kate Houston Mitchoff, Melody Allen, Elizabeth K. Bush, Sarah English, Wendy Lukehart, Penny Peck, Linda Plevak, Rebecca Purdy, and Jewell Stoddard

SCS
MS
10
04
05